ZOOBOTS

Wild Robots Inspired by Real Animals

WRITTEN BY **Helaine Becker**

ILLUSTRATED BY **Alex Ries**

Kids Can Press

For Android Robot and Snikes — H.B.

For my parents, Alma and Peter — A.R.

Acknowledgments

Shrewbot: Bristol Robotics Lab, Bristol, UK; **Uncle Sam:** Carnegie Mellon Biorobotics Lab, Pittsburgh, PA; **Whitesides Color Changer**: Whitesides Research Group, Harvard University, Cambridge, MA (with special thanks to George Whitesides); **Octobot:** The BioRobotics Institute, Scuola Superiore Sant'Anna, Pisa, Italy; **Ole Pill Bug:** University of Magdeburg-Stendal, Germany; **Stickybot III:** Biomimetics and Dexterous Manipulation, Stanford University, Palo Alto, CA and Biomimetic Millisystems Laboratory, University of California, Berkeley; **Ghostbot:** McCormick School of Engineering and Applied Science, Northwestern University, Chicago, IL; **Nanobot:** NanoRobotics Laboratory, École Polytechnique de Montréal, Montreal, QC (with special thanks to Sylvain Martel); **Robobat:** North Carolina State University, Raleigh, NC and University of Michigan College of Engineering, Ann Arbor, MI; **DASH:** Free University of Brussels, Brussels, Belgium; **Air Jelly** and **AquaJelly:** Festo AG & Co., Esslingen, Germany; **Geminoid F:** Geminoid F was developed by Osaka University and Hiroshi Ishiguro Laboratory, Advanced Telecommunications Research Institute International (ATR).

Text © 2014 Helaine Becker
Illustrations © 2014 Alex Ries

Kids Can Press acknowledges the financial support of the Government of Ontario, through the Ontario Media Development Corporation's Ontario Book Initiative; the Ontario Arts Council; the Canada Council for the Arts; and the Government of Canada, through the CBF, for our publishing activity.

Published in Canada by
Kids Can Press Ltd.
25 Dockside Drive
Toronto, ON M5A 0B5

Published in the U.S. by
Kids Can Press Ltd.
2250 Military Road
Tonawanda, NY 14150

www.kidscanpress.com

The artwork in this book was rendered in Photoshop CS5.
The text is set in Eurostile.

Edited by Karen Li and Stacey Roderick
Designed by Julia Naimska

This book is smyth sewn casebound.
Manufactured in Shenzhen, China, in 10/2013 by C & C Offset.

CM 14 0 9 8 7 6 5 4 3 2 1

Library and Archives Canada Cataloguing in Publication

Becker, Helaine, 1961-, author
        Zoobots : wild robots inspired by real animals / written by Helaine Becker; illustrated by Alex Ries.

Includes index.
ISBN 978-1-55453-971-0 (bound)

1. Robots — Juvenile literature. 2. Animal behavior — Juvenile literature.
I. Ries, Alex, illustrator II. Title.

TJ211.2.B42 2014   j629.8'92   C2013-905301-8

Kids Can Press is a **CORUS**™ Entertainment company

CONTENTS

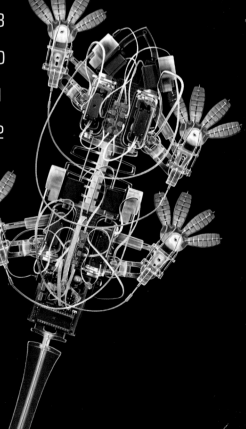

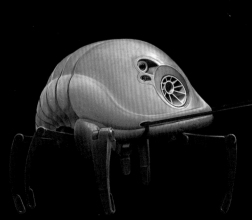

WILD ABOUT ROBOTS!

Imagine a thrilling otherworld populated by invincible robot animals. These fierce zoobots would have freaky superpowers, such as the ability to walk up walls. They'd fly on wings of steel. They'd slither on silicone skin. They'd march through searing flames wearing fireproof armor.

   Amazing ... and true: these bizarre robo-animals are actually being developed by today's most daring roboticists. Using mechatronics — mechanical and electrical engineering combined with computer science — they are designing and building wild, animal-inspired robots right here on Earth!

   Real-life zoobots are built to solve particular problems and perform specific tasks. They

can do things humans can't. They can plunge to the depths of the sea and tunnel into the chambers of your body. They can sniff out toxic gases and help rescue accident victims.

On the pages of this book, you will come eyeball to eyeball with some of the creepiest, crawliest and downright weirdest real-life robots ever invented. You will find out about the challenges they were each designed to solve. You will also get the inside scoop on how nature inspired their wild designs.

Last but not least, you'll get a sneak peek at what's coming soon to a robot zoo near you. What might the next generation of uber-beasts be able to do? To find out, enter the zoobot zoo here (if you dare) ...

SNUUURRRFF!

NAME: Shrewbot

TEAM: Terra

REALM: Mammalia

SUPER SKILL:

The ability to determine the position, shape and texture of objects using computerized "whiskers"

SPECIFICATIONS:

- Functions in dark, dusty or smoke-filled areas where vision is difficult
- Can make rapid-fire decisions about the identities and locations of objects
- Can create detailed maps of unfamiliar environments

APPLICATIONS:

- For search-and-rescue operations, such as finding survivors of a fire
- As bomb sniffers
- To map hidden areas, such as ancient Egyptian tombs or underwater caves
- To inspect materials, such as textiles, for flaws or damage

EVOLVED FROM:

The Etruscan Pygmy Shrew
The Etruscan pygmy shrew is an excellent hunter that feeds on a wide variety of small animals, such as insects, earthworms and frogs, many of which may be larger than it is!

Since it is nocturnal, the shrew relies on its super-sensitive whiskers to find prey in the dark. It sweeps its whiskers back and forth at high speed to sense vibrations (tiny movements back and forth or up and down) from the environment. The shrew uses the vibrations to target the location of a prey animal and the direction of its movement.

The Shrewbot, like its Etruscan pygmy shrew "ancestor," can move its snout independently of its body. This allows its whiskers to "sweep" a wide area and home in on its target. Each whisker can also move on its own, giving the Shrewbot's nose even more flexibility and sniff range. Because it can detect and identify objects through "active touch," the Shrewbot can be sent places where visual surveillance is otherwise impossible, such as dark or smoke-filled rooms.

whisker

STATUS UPDATE:
Working prototype

SLITHER!

NAME: Uncle Sam

TEAM: Terra

REALM: Reptilia

SUPER SKILL:

Can shape-shift and move on both land and water

SPECIFICATIONS:

- Can climb up otherwise impossible surfaces, such as inside hollow pipes or ductwork
- Is ideal for surveillance — its camera "eye" can detect targets and send information back to monitoring stations
- Is virtually indestructible — can survive a 3 m (10 ft.) drop
- Is waterproof

APPLICATIONS:

- To perform search-and-rescue operations, such as locating trapped earthquake victims
- To reach difficult-to-access locations and bring back objects
- To perform surgical exploration of human organs, such as the heart
- To lift and place heavy parts on assembly lines

EVOLVED FROM:

The Snake

Snakes are essentially compact tubes of powerful muscle. By contracting and relaxing the muscles in sequence, snakes can conquer virtually any terrain. They can creep, slither, slide, sidewind (move sideways) and swim; they can twist, loop, roll, flex and ripple. They can wrap themselves around trees or strangle prey within their powerful coils.

The serpentine zoobot is built from repeating sections of sensors and actuators (moving parts). Each section is able to sense its surroundings and move on its own. The zoobot's length and function can be altered by adding or taking away sections. When multiple components are combined, the zoobot can twist, turn, loop and ripple in virtually every direction, much like a living snake. The sneakiest Uncle Sams can actually put themselves together in the field!

STATUS UPDATE:
Working prototype

STALK!

NAME: Whitesides' Color Changer

TEAM: Marina

REALM: Cephalopoda

SUPER SKILL:

Able to hide and disguise itself in wide-ranging conditions

SPECIFICATIONS:

- Has a soft, squishy body
- Can change color to match or stand out from a background, making observation and retrieval easy
- Can glow in the dark
- Can grasp delicate objects without breaking them

APPLICATIONS:

- To sneak into enemy territory unseen and conduct surveillance missions
- For observing in public places where it would be useful to remain unnoticed
- As a visual marker to help emergency personnel in search-and-rescue missions
- To cross gooey or sticky areas (due to its light weight and flexibility)

EVOLVED FROM:

The Starfish
Starfish are not fish at all, but members of the Echinoderm family. They "walk" across the ocean floor using tube feet — soft, squishy tubes that expand and contract to grip and release the ground in waves. The tube feet can also grasp prey with strength and delicacy, allowing the starfish to pry open shellfish such as oysters and eat the soft food within.

The Cuttlefish

Cuttlefish have the ability to change their color to match the background. They do so by expanding and contracting pockets of color, called chromatophores, in their skin. Cuttlefish use color to camouflage themselves and hide from both prey and predators.

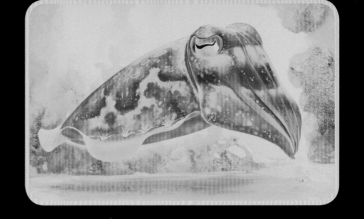

SPECIAL OPS:

The Whitesides' Color Changer combines the best features of a starfish's movement with a cuttlefish's amazing camouflage ability. The rubbery, four-legged Whitesides' robots are made out of a silicone-based polymer. When dye is forced through channels in the robot's skin, the color changes to either match its surroundings or to stand out as a "flag" for observers. Glow-in-the-dark ink can be used so the robot is seen at night or in dark spaces.

Hot or cold liquids can also be forced through the channels, changing the robot's temperature. This enables the robot to hide from infrared detectors that look for heat changes in a given area.

The robot's unique method of locomotion, borrowed from the starfish, enables it to walk across rough or sticky terrain. It can also hold very delicate objects, such as uncooked eggs or even live mice!

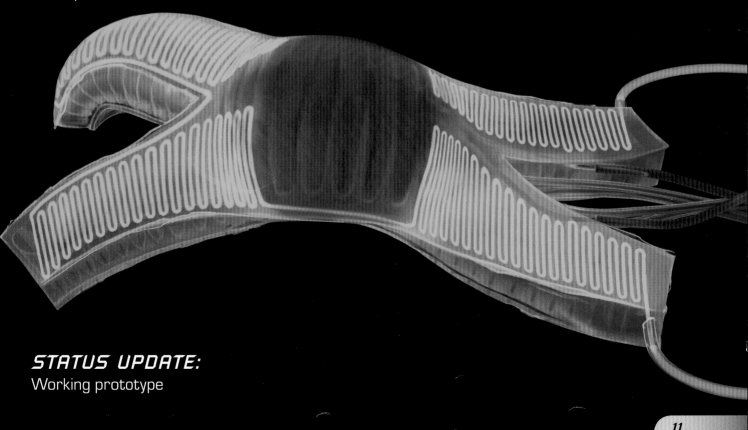

STATUS UPDATE:
Working prototype

SQUEEZE!

NAME: Octobot

TEAM: Marina

REALM: Cephalopoda

SUPER SKILL:

Shape-shifter that can assume virtually any shape and can grip almost any object

SPECIFICATIONS:

- Can squeeze its soft body into narrow crevices
- Can wrap firmly around objects
- Hundreds of suckers provide a grip of steel

APPLICATIONS:

- Search and rescue in marine environments
- Delicate surgical procedures by being threaded into small openings in the human body
- Underwater exploration, particularly of the ocean floor (e.g., shipwrecks)

EVOLVED FROM:

The Mediterranean Octopus
Octopi are widely considered to be among the smartest of marine dwellers. Their nerve cells are not concentrated in their brain like humans but are distributed throughout their body. That means that their arms are able to think — and act — independently.

Their arms are composed entirely of muscle, without bones to support them. When filled with water, the muscle cells become super strong and rigid. When water is released, they collapse and soften. The octopus adjusts water pressure and volume in its muscles to become virtually any shape, from a soft, squishy disk to a rigid tube.

The Octobot's soft, rubbery silicone skin is wrapped around a central steel cable with nylon cables attached to it. Like muscle fibers, the cables can flex or tighten when electric current is applied. This gives the Octobot the same shape-shifting abilities as its biological kin. It can grasp objects tightly and also squeeze into nooks and crannies to reach places humans or other machines can't. Each arm, like that of real octopi, is able to operate independently for greater range and flexibility.

STATUS UPDATE:
Prototype in development

SPRAY!

NAME: Ole Pill Bug

TEAM: Terra

REALM: Crustacea

SUPER SKILL:

Can withstand high temperatures and put out fires

SPECIFICATIONS:

- Has heat-resistant, overlapping armor plating
- Equipped with tanks of water and powdered fire-extinguishing agents
- Detects heat from a fire from up to 800 m (½ mi.) away, and travels at speeds of up to 20 km (12½ mi.) per hour
- Uses GPS (Global Positioning System) and feelers with infrared heat sensors to beeline directly toward a raging forest fire
- Can be placed near target sites in a dormant state, for use as needed

APPLICATIONS:

- To fight forest fires
- To reduce fire danger in war zones
- To surprise the enemy in an advance attack wave, ahead of human combatants

EVOLVED FROM:

The Pill Bug

Pill bugs, or roly-polies, are a land-living form of crustacean related to lobsters. Overlapping scales of a tough material called chitin act like body armor. When threatened, the pill bug rolls itself into a small ball, so it is completely covered by its impenetrable armor. With its seven pairs of legs, the pill bug is extremely agile and fast moving.

Much larger than its crustacean counterpart, the 91 kg (200 lb.) Ole zoobot has armor plating made of fire-resistant ceramic fiber compounds. It can withstand withering heat of up to 1010°C/1850°F — the temperature of freshly spewed lava.

Ole's six sturdy legs are ideally suited for crossing the burning terrain found in forest fires or on battlegrounds. Unlike wheels, which remain in contact with the ground at all times, Ole's legs touch down only for a short time. That lets them stay cool enough to keep operating, even in extreme heat conditions.

Working together, 30 pill bug zoobots could protect a forest area measuring a whopping 6995 km^2 (2700 sq. mi.).

STATUS UPDATE:
Working prototype

STICK!

NAME: Stickybot III

TEAM: Terra

REALM: Reptilia

SUPER SKILL:

Can harness powerful atomic forces to achieve super stickiness

SPECIFICATIONS:

- Can climb smooth surfaces humans or traditional machines can't reach
- Can easily detach from any surface without leaving slime or sticky residue
- Can change directions using rotating ankles and interchangeable feet
- Can climb at 3 m (118 in.) per minute

APPLICATIONS:

- To reach difficult-to-get-to areas like exterior walls of skyscrapers or inside mine shafts
- To perform surveillance and reconnaissance
- Scaled up for use in human-size robots, the technology might allow people to climb walls like a comic strip superhero

EVOLVED FROM:

The Gecko

Geckos are nocturnal lizards. Many species have specialized toe pads covered in tiny ridges that are called lamellae. The lamellae are furred with millions of hairs, called setae. The setae's small size allows them to use a microscopic yet powerful force called van der Waals force. The force physically bonds, or joins, the setae to the molecules on the climbing surface. The bond is broken when the gecko lifts its foot. The gecko can therefore walk on any surface without using sticky adhesive.

toe pad

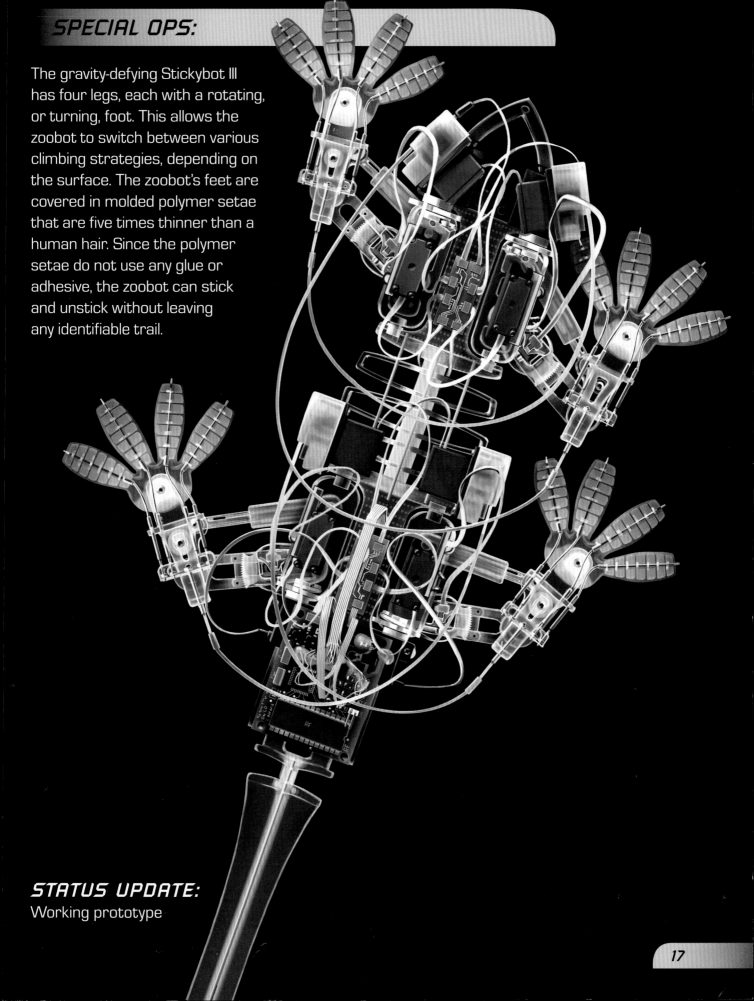

The gravity-defying Stickybot III has four legs, each with a rotating, or turning, foot. This allows the zoobot to switch between various climbing strategies, depending on the surface. The zoobot's feet are covered in molded polymer setae that are five times thinner than a human hair. Since the polymer setae do not use any glue or adhesive, the zoobot can stick and unstick without leaving any identifiable trail.

STATUS UPDATE:
Working prototype

RIPPLE!

NAME: Ghostbot

TEAM: Marina

REALM: Piscina

SUPER SKILL:

Can swim in any direction using a rippling, ribbon-like fin

SPECIFICATIONS:

- Ribbon-like fin made up of 32 artificial fin rays, each powered by a waterproof motor and independently controlled
- Ultra-flexible for movement in almost any direction
- Electro-sensors throughout enable it to act like a single large eye

APPLICATIONS:

- To study coral reefs
- To perform search-and-rescue operations
- To act as a motor to propel underwater vehicles
- To reach deep, underwater oil wells and fix oil spills
- To monitor ocean pollution

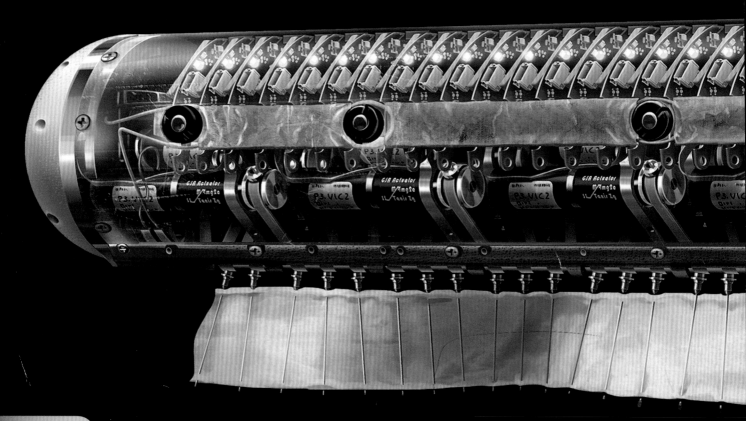

EVOLVED FROM:

The Black Ghost Knifefish

This dark dweller of the deep doesn't have the familiar fins of a common fish. Instead, the black ghost knifefish gets its name from a single, rippling fin along its belly. With extreme precision, the knifefish can slide through the murky waters of the Amazon and sneak up on prey from virtually any direction — vertically, horizontally and diagonally. The black ghost knifefish can then stun its unsuspecting prey with a self-generated electrical charge, making it doubly deadly.

SPECIAL OPS:

The Ghostbot mimics the real fish's fluttering fin to achieve incredible flexibility. Electro-sensors packed throughout the Ghostbot turn it into an all-powerful surveillance tool that can hover over rough terrain, such as shipwrecks, underwater oil or gas wells, and coral reefs. The robotic eyes scan the target and send data, such as the object's condition or placement, back to monitoring stations.

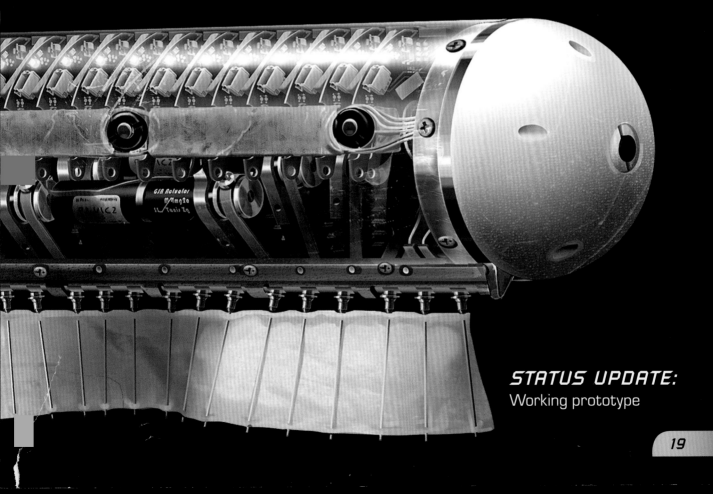

STATUS UPDATE:
Working prototype

WHIP!

NAME: Nanobot

TEAM: Micro

REALM: Bacteria

SUPER SKILL:

Rapid-snap whiptails enable locomotion at a microscopic level

SPECIFICATIONS:

- Microscopic
- Guided locomotion
- Powered by internal chemical molecular motors
- Capable of working together in huge numbers to move microscopic objects

APPLICATIONS:

- To deliver cancer-fighting drugs deep within the human body
- To build microscopic "machines" used in computer components
- To detect leaks in spacecraft and nuclear power stations

EVOLVED FROM:

Bacteria

Bacteria are single-celled organisms too small to be seen by the naked eye. They reproduce rapidly to form huge colonies, or groups. Bacteria can communicate, so they can work together.

Certain types of bacteria, such as *Serratia marcescens*, can swim rapidly using whip-like tails called flagellae. The flagellae twist like corkscrews, first in one direction and then the other, for exceptional agility and speed.

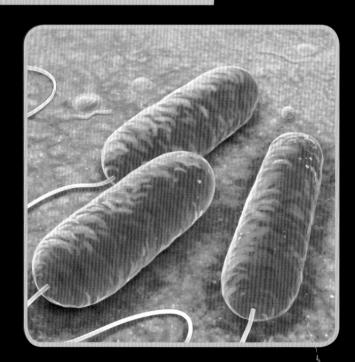

SPECIAL OPS:

Nanobots are hybrids made of bacteria and mini-machines joined together. The machines are programmed to instruct the bacteria how to move. The bacteria then use their flagellae to propel themselves and the object they are attached to. Working as a group, they can move objects much larger than themselves.

In addition, because they can communicate with one another, Nanobot colonies can act like a single unit. With scarily mindless efficiency, the colonies can be directed to perform tasks such as building materials (like microscopic computer components), delivering life-saving chemicals through blood vessels or exploring areas beyond the scope of human travel, such as far-flung planets.

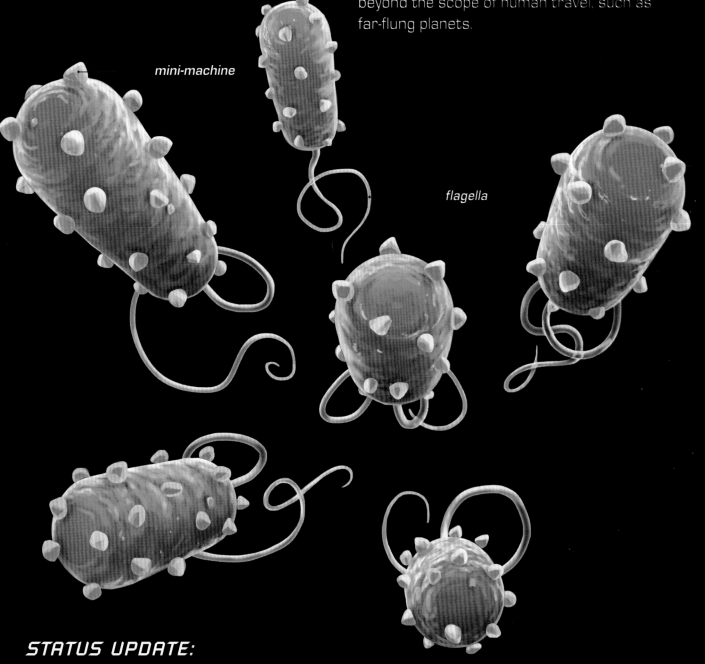

mini-machine

flagella

STATUS UPDATE:
Working prototype

SWOOP!

NAME: Robobat

TEAM: Terra

REALM: Mammalia

SUPER SKILL:

Flight enabled by rapid-snap, shape-shifting wings

SPECIFICATIONS:

- Superior movement and aerodynamics
- Power generated from the sun and wind
- Equipped with cameras and microphones for two-way communication
- Wings made from a combination of stretchy synthetic material, steel and a super-elastic metal alloy that provides a full range of motion and always snaps back to its original position

APPLICATIONS:

- To perform surveillance and reconnaissance, especially in urban combat zones and disaster areas
- To detect danger from nuclear fallout, biological weapons or toxic gas

EVOLVED FROM:

The Bat

Bats have ultra-powerful, ultra-flexible wings that are unique in the animal kingdom. Each wing is like a morphed hand. The elongated finger bones have less calcium near their tips. This makes the bones unusually light and flexible.

The fingers are covered in a thin, stretchy membrane — like very thin skin — coated with cells that are highly sensitive to touch. Air flowing over them provides detailed data about wind speed and direction. The bat can respond by subtly adjusting its wings to achieve maximum speed and efficiency.

Robobat's wings are composed of an artificial, stretchy skin that is thinner than a sheet of paper. The skin is stretched over specially engineered joints made from a metal alloy. The joints snap back and forth between two basic shapes when they are heated by an electric current (sent by an onboard battery). The joints' shape-changing ability allows the featherlight wings to flap up and down like a bat's wing.

Real bats navigate and find prey using echolocation (following the way sound bounces off an object). Robobat uses low-power radar for the same purpose. Additional sensors could include tiny stereo cameras, microphones, radiation detectors

and poisonous gas detectors. They would make Robobat the perfect "Dark Drone" for dangerous missions — a remote-controlled, miniature spy plane that sees all without being seen and without risking human life.

STATUS UPDATE:
Prototype in development

CREEP!

 NAME: **DASH** (Dynamic Autonomous Sprawled Hexapod)

 REALM: Insecta

TEAM: Terra

SUPER SKILL:

Tactical intelligence through mind control

SPECIFICATIONS:

- Are self-programming
- Can communicate among themselves using radio frequencies and electronic sensors
- Can work as a coordinated force
- Are small, inexpensive and sturdy

APPLICATIONS:

- For search-and-rescue operations
- To modify the behavior of other animals
- To explore and infiltrate enemy bunkers
- To transmit video and other data to a home base

EVOLVED FROM:

The Cockroach

These highly social insects have existed since the age of dinosaurs. They possess a staggering array of survival tools that have

enabled them to infiltrate and conquer habitats worldwide. They are equipped with an indestructible, tank-like build and an impressive scuttle speed of 75 cm (29½ in.) per second. They can also communicate among themselves using chemical signals called pheromones.

Most importantly, when cockroaches gather in large groups, a powerful trait called "swarm intelligence" or "collective intelligence" emerges. It allows the group to act like a single-minded organism, in a purposeful way, without any controller or leader.

Cockroach-inspired zoobots are programmed with AI (artificial intelligence) software to "think" and "problem solve." While each individual zoobot has only a limited skill set, Wi-Fi communication between individuals allows the zoobots to work together to perform an intelligent, purposeful action. Swarms can be sent to remote locations, where, as a group, they can identify the problem to be solved (following a guiding principle, such as "locate fallen soldiers") and develop strategies to achieve the desired outcome (such as "radio GPS coordinates to a base command").

Robotic cockroaches can also influence the behavior of real cockroaches. For example, since cockroaches are social animals, they tend to gather together. So when robotic cockroaches are programmed to gather in brightly lit areas, real cockroaches will join them, even though they normally prefer the dark! This ability will allow other zoobots based on cockroaches to perform a wide variety of "crowd control" tasks.

STATUS UPDATE:
Working prototype

SWARM!

NAME: **AirJelly** and **AquaJelly**

TEAM: Marina

REALM: Cnidaria

SUPER SKILL:

Swarming using lighter-than-air flight and marine locomotion (the ability to move from one place to another)

SPECIFICATIONS:

- Can move through air or water in virtually any direction
- Can communicate with monitoring stations and other jellies to effect coordinated swarming action

APPLICATIONS:

- To herd other bots or life-forms into a designated area
- To transport, e.g., underwater vehicles or air travel
- To garner data and engage in reconnaissance

EVOLVED FROM:

The Jellyfish
Jellyfish are incredible survival artists. Fossils dating back more than 500 million years indicate that the jellyfish design — a floating, goo-filled sac with trailing toxic tentacles — is both versatile and efficient. Jellyfish are also ferocious hunters and can form large swarms to overpower prey.

AirJellies and AquaJellies apply the time-tested body plan of jellyfish to achieve superior movement in air and water. They propel their balloon-like bodies by contracting and relaxing their tentacles in waves. They can steer themselves by shifting the position of a central pendulum. AirJellies use a short-range radio system to communicate among themselves and to initiate swarm behavior. In water, AquaJellies use pulsing LED lights that can be read by other AquaJellies.

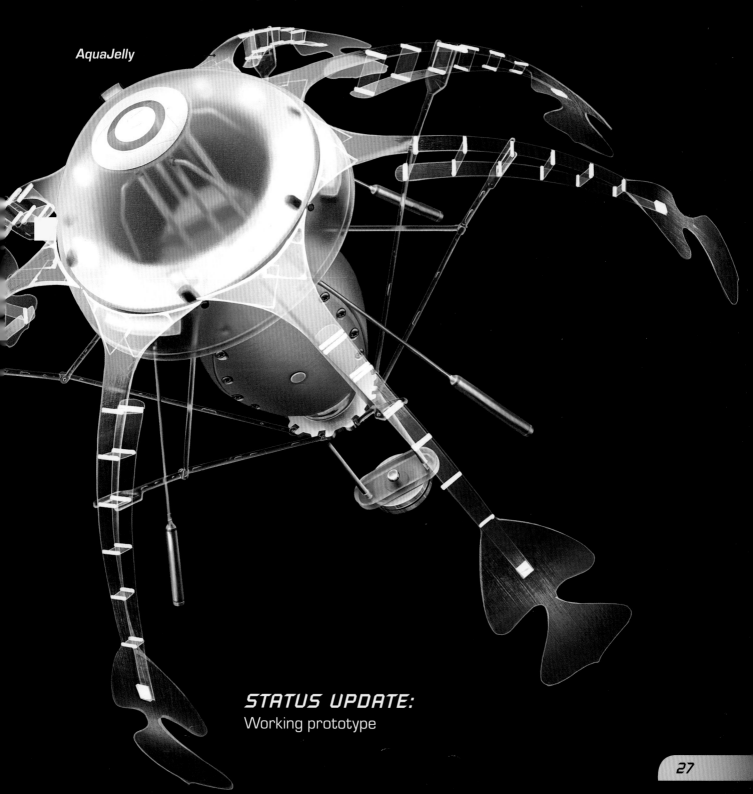

AquaJelly

STATUS UPDATE:
Working prototype

NAME: Geminoid F

TEAM: Terra

REALM: Mammalia

SUPER SKILL:

Can infiltrate human society with deceptively lifelike appearance and behavior

SPECIFICATIONS:

- Full-size, lifelike human appearance, complete with realistic skin, eyebrows, eyelashes and fingernails
- Human-like movement, including naturalistic eye motion and subtle head and hand motions
- Can read and respond to human facial expressions with uncanny accuracy
- Cameras in eyes allow it to see and send visual data back to its operator

APPLICATIONS:

- On spy missions where the potential for the loss of human life is high
- In medical facilities as nurses during outbreaks of contagious diseases

EVOLVED FROM:

The Human Being
Human beings are a species of primate that possesses high intelligence. A very social species, humans are extremely effective at communicating using vocalizations, gestures and facial expressions. Humans are very adaptable and can flourish in virtually any habitat. This unique animal also has the rare ability to tame other species, both plant and animal, to serve its needs.

SPECIAL OPS:

When controlled by a remote operator, Geminoid F can mimic the appearance and behavior of human beings. It can blink, shift its eyes, turn its neck, appear to breathe, bend over as if to bow and speak. It can detect the individual facial expressions and head movements of a real human, then reproduce them to seem like a real member of the group. This ability is especially effective when the zoobot is observed remotely using telecommunication devices, such as a Skype portal. Geminoid F's high level of realism enables it to communicate persuasively with humans and to copy their behavior.

STATUS UPDATE:
Working prototype

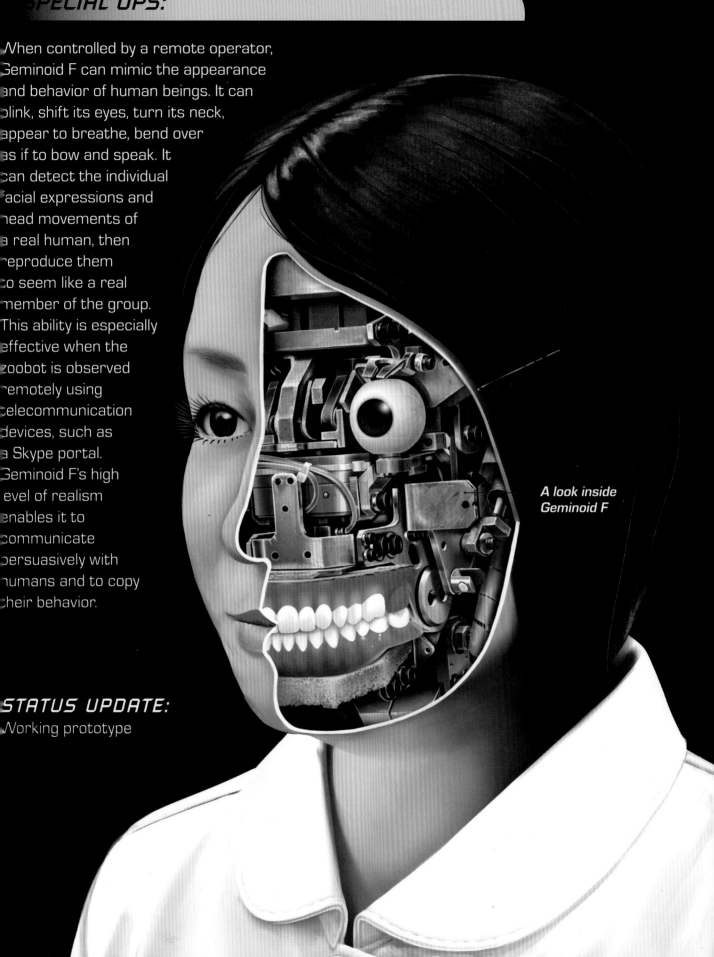

A look inside Geminoid F

ZOOBOT FUTURE?

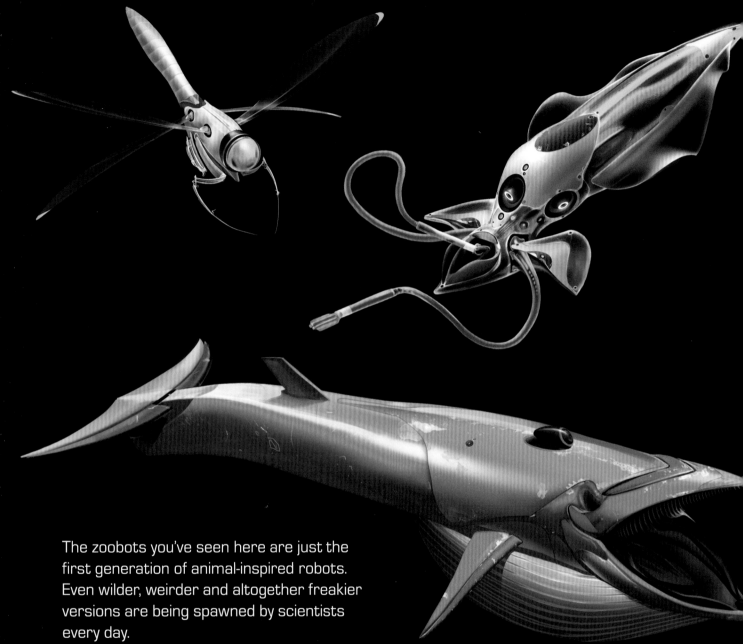

The zoobots you've seen here are just the first generation of animal-inspired robots. Even wilder, weirder and altogether freakier versions are being spawned by scientists every day.

Soon there might be stealthy stingray zoobots to monitor underwater shorelines. Next there might be remote-controlled sand flea "tanks" that can leap straight up in the air and over obstacles. Or there might be fierce cheetahbots, with ultra-flexible metal spines, that can run like the wind.

Will zoobots like Dragonfly drones, Krakenbots or Whalebots eventually take over this world? Perhaps. But then again, perhaps they already have …

GLOSSARY

Aerodynamics — the science of how air and the solid objects moving through it behave

Alloy — a metal made by combining two or more other metals

Artificial Intelligence (AI) — the study and design of computer systems that can perform tasks that, to date, have required human thinking and perceptual skills such as reasoning and object recognition

Bacteria — microscopic single-celled organisms

Cephalopoda — marine mollusks, such as octopi, squid and cuttlefish, with large heads, large eyes, tentacles and ink sacs for defense

Chitin — the tough, protective, semitransparent material that makes up the exoskeletons (or outside skeleton) of arthropods (insects, crustaceans, etc.)

Crustacea — the class of animals that includes lobsters, crabs, shrimps, barnacles and pill bugs. Characteristics include a hard exoskeleton (or outside skeleton), segmented body and paired, jointed legs.

Echolocation — the use of sound waves to locate an object. Bats use echolocation to navigate and find prey.

Electro-sensors — electronic devices used to detect specific stimuli: sights, smells, sounds, motion, chemicals, etc.

Flagellae — whip-like tails belonging to a variety of single-celled organisms and used for locomotion

Hybrid — a mixture of two or more parts, usually referring to a plant or animal bred from parents of different species

Infiltrate — to secretly gain access to an organization or location

Lamellae — thin, foldable layers

LED — light-emitting diode, a form of high-efficiency lighting

Locomotion — the ability to move from one place to another under one's own power

Mammalia — warm-blooded higher vertebrates, such as humans, that feed their young with milk from mammary glands

Mechatronics — an area of engineering that combines mechanical and electrical engineering with computer science

Membrane — a thin sheet or layer that acts as a boundary between regions or materials

Molecule — the smallest fundamental unit of a chemical compound. Made up of a group of atoms, bonded together.

Nocturnal — active at night

Organism — a living creature: a plant, animal, fungi or protozoan

Pheromone — a chemical secreted by an animal, especially an insect, that influences the behavior of others of the same species

Polymer — a chemical compound made up of repeating structural elements

Reconaissance — military observation of a specific area in order to locate an enemy or determine strategic features

Roboticist — an engineer who designs and builds robots

Setae — tiny bristles or hairs

Silicone — a synthetic, rubbery, durable compound made from silicon and oxygen mixed with other chemicals

Surveillance — close observation, usually of a criminal suspect or enemy

van der Waals force — the force that contributes to bonding between molecules